I AM
Manifesto

In loving memory of my beautiful son Gabriel, my muse forever

SB Hilarion

For My Children

and

ALL the Children of the World

"Our first teacher is our own heart."—Cheyenne proverb

Acknowledgements to Miguel, my anchor and my love for over twenty-five years, my brother Chad, Maksym Turkot, Angie Gruber, Maria Mazzara, Sheila Hilton, Lily Ying Meng, Stacey Jones, Najya Williams, and Anastasia Turkot. Thank you all so much for your support, critique and guidance. Angie, I appreciate that you're on this journey with me. Maksym, you are such a gifted artist and a true philomath. I look forward to collaborating more with you via our "language translator," your dad Oleksiy.

Please visit us at www.SBHilarion.com!

RYSS

I AM

Manifesto

SB Hilarion

Hello philomaths*!

I am Hao Finley (HF) Lee, and I am Sabine Yi (SY) Lee.

In I AM Manifesto, for every day of the calendar year, there is a different word

for each mantra or affirmation:

"I am _____ that I am."

You can create your own mantras. But we've given you a good list using every

letter of the alphabet from which to choose!

You can say the mantra "assigned" for each day of the year, repeating it as often

as you wish. We like to repeat ours three times twice a day.

You can select one or a few for each month or for the entire year.

We've chosen the mantras we'd like to affirm monthly for our own journey.

Wherever you see a picture, that represents our mantra!

We hope the mantras build your self-esteem and belief in yourself. We hope

these mantras empower you.

At the same time,you expand your knowledge with some humongous and cool words,

along with us.

This is your manifesto, fellow philomath.

There isn't a right way or a wrong way, or a better way or a worse way.

There is just Your Way.

It's all up to YOU!

SAY it. BELIEVE it. BECOME it. MANIFEST it.

See you soon!

Hao Finley and *Sabine Yi (HF&SY)*

* A PHILOMATH is "a seeker of knowledge; a person who loves learning and studying new facts and acquiring new knowledge."
The official name for what you already are!

"I AM

QUIESCENT TODAY.

I need to rest, not too much play.

I am that I am."

Hao Finley, Sabine Yi

January

I AM _____ that I am.

I AM	I AM	I AM	I AM	I AM	I AM	I AM
1* Compassionate	2 Motivated	3 Intelligent	4 Healthy	5* Jovial	6* Stalwart	7* having an Auspicious year
8 Nice	9* Resourceful	10* Complimentary	11 Well-meaning	12 Visible	13 Adventurous	14* Quiescent today
15 Fearless	16 Enough	17* Percipient	18 True	19 Levelheaded	20 Youthful	21 Cuddly
22* Spry	23 Beautiful	24 Generous	25 Dependable	26 Expressive	27 Unbreakable	28* Zealous
29 Open-minded	30 Polite	31 Knowledgeable				

"I AM

DISCIPLINED.

I will achieve my goals again and again.

I am that I am."

Hao Finley

February

I AM _____ that I am.

I AM	I AM	I AM	I AM	I AM	I AM	I AM
1 Smart	2* Ambitious	3 Respectful	4 Centered	5* Eloquent	6 Observant	7 Making time for Me
8* Impassioned	9* Versatile	10 Affectionate	11 Belonging	12 Strong 自弓虫	13 Humorous	14 Loved
15 Praiseworthy	16 Glowing	17 Calm	18* Disciplined	19* Astute	20 Fair	21 Tolerant
22 Charitable	23 Understanding	24 World.ly	25* Tactful	26* Meticulous	27 Patient	28 Neat
Leap Year 29* Affable						

"I AM

STUDIOUS.

With so much out there, how can I not be curious?

I am that I am."

Sabine Yi

"I AM **QUALIFIED**
to be a philomath's guide
on this journey worldwide." Sabine Yi

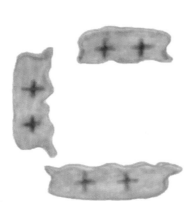

March

I AM _____ that I am.

I AM	I AM	I AM	I AM	I AM	I AM	I AM
1* Circumspect	2 Effective	3* Frugal	4 Mannerly	5 Approachable	6 Studious	7 Gracious
8* Dauntless	9 Rational	10 Advancing	11 Precise	12 Confident	13 Innovative	14* Judicious
15* Witty	16 Talented	17 Leading by good example	18 Enlivened	19 Investing in myself, and...	20* Fecund	21 Nurturing
22 Positive thinking	23 Goal-oriented	24 Qualified	25* Resilient	26 Serene	27 Open-hearted	28* Hospitable
29* Altruistic	30* Contemplative	31 Blessed				

"I AM

STRENGHTENING MYSELF MENTALLY.

Bullies and tyrants make me believe MORE in Myself daily.

I am that I am."

Hao Finley

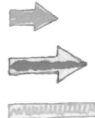

April

I AM _____ that I am.

I AM	I AM	I AM	I AM	I AM	I AM	I AM
1* Genteel	2 Assertive	3* Upright	4 Improving	5* Blissful	6* Valiant	7* Empathic
8 Proactive	9* Comely	10 Respectable	11 Teachable	12 Invigorated	13 Moved	14 Flourishing
15 Strengthening myself	16 Well-disposed	17 Hearing	18 Listening (well)	19 Grateful	20* Discreet	21 Contributing
22 Courteous	23* Sagacious	24* Expeditious	25 Able	26* Pacific	27 On the right foot	28 Worthy
29 Affirming	30 Forward looking					

"I AM

SHARING.

My family teaches me to be generous and caring.

I am that I am."

Sabine Yi

May

I AM _____ that I am.

I AM	I AM	I AM	I AM	I AM	I AM	I AM
1* Optimistic	2 Au fait (= fully informed)	3* Vocal	4* Erudite	5 Playful	6 Nourished	7 Making a difference
8* Conscientious	9 Questioning	10 Aware	11 Independent	12* Dignified	13* Zestful	14 Relaxed
15 Making time for...	16 Sharing	17* Polished	18 Wise	19 Good	20* Empowered	21* Tenacious
22 Genuine	23 Humble	24* Fruitful	25 Artistic	26 Brave	27 Laughing	28 Constructive
29 Prepared	30 Decisive	31 Successful				

"I AM

TIMELY.

I am sharing knowledge,
not late or too early.

I am that I am."

Hao Finley, Sabine Yi

*"I AM LIFE. Positive energy
helps me thrive."* Mommy Lee

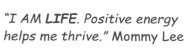

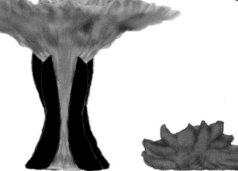

June

I AM _____ that I am.

I AM	I AM	I AM	I AM	I AM	I AM	I AM
1 Appreciated	2 Well-behaved	3* Economical	4 Innocent	5 Considerate	6 Timely	7* Poised
8* Modest	9* Competent	10* Objective	11 Bright	12 Honorable	13 Virtuous	14 Fulfilled
15 Handsome	16* Attentive	17* Discerning	18 Conversant	19* Responsible	20 Giving	21 Revitalized
22 Positive Energy	23* Equable	24* Jocose	25 Good-natured	26 Sympathetic	27 Keen	28* Artisanal
29 Insightful	30 Life					

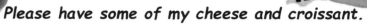

"I AM

ABUNDANT.

Please have some of my cheese and croissant.

I am that I am."

Sabine Yi

July

I AM _____ that I am.

I AM	I AM	I AM	I AM	I AM	I AM	I AM
1 Outgoing	2 Courageous	3 Refreshed	4 Lively	5 Free	6* Unique	7 Adorable
8 Whole	9 Determined	10* Personable	11 Honest	12* Intrepid	13 Scholarly	14 Enlightened
15 Creative	16* Genial	17 Abundant	18 Selfless	19* Jocular	20 Thoughtful	21 Balanced
22* Intuitive	23 Philosophical	24* Charismatic	25* Earnest	26 Multi-dimensional	27* Galvanized	28 Natural
29* Magnanimous	30 Amiable	31 Fortunate				

"I AM

COMMUNICATIVE.

I am hearing and listening well,
so I can be more expansive.

I am that I am."

Hao Finley

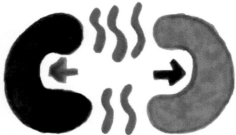

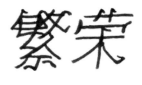

繁荣

August

I AM _____ that I am.

I AM	I AM	I AM	I AM	I AM	I AM	I AM
1 Stable	2 Communicative	3 Interested in...	4 Hopeful	5 Exultant	6 Lucky	7 Rejuvenated
8 Welcoming	9* Authentic	10 Sensible	11 Decent	12* Blithe	13 Up to par	14 Capable
15 Fun	16 Incentivized	17* Animated	18 OKAY	19* Perspicacious	20 Elevated	21 Just
22* Prosperous	23 Valued	24* Guileless	25 Mature	26* Dexterous	27 Chipper	28 Tough
29 Active	30* Qui vive	31* Triumphant				

"I AM

FOCUSED.

Quiet as a mouse with no ruckus.

I am that I am."

Sabine Yi

Commodities

Equities ← ↑ → Cash

Toys ← $ → Books

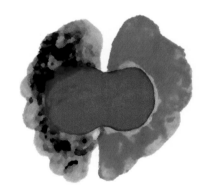

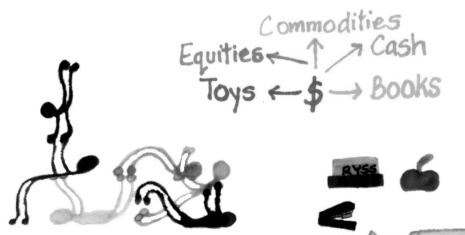

September

I AM _____ that I am.

I AM	I AM	I AM	I AM	I AM	I AM	I AM
1 Admirable	2 Efficient	3* Jocund	4 Cultured	5* Benevolent	6 Organized	7* Noble
8 Learning	9 Mindful	10 Embracing others	11* Persevering	12 Renewed	13 Cordial	14* Scrupulous
15 Well-advised	16* Punctual	17* Gutsy	18 Aspiring (to …)	19* Cerebral	20 Real	21 Inspired & Inspiring
22 Hilarious	23* Attuned	24* Unflappable	25 Focused	26 Driven	27* Zippy	28* Prudent
29 Tidy	30 Skillful					

"I AM

LIONHEARTED.

I'm very young, but not easily thwarted.

I am that I am."

Sabine Yi

FOOD

"I am *HUMANITARIAN*.
I don't need praise
to help other children." Hao Finley

1

真诚

October

I AM _____ that I am.

I AM	I AM	I AM	I AM	I AM	I AM	I AM
1* Lionhearted	2 Civil	3 One with all	4 Articulate	5 Influential	6* Winsome	7* Urbane
8 Friendly	9* Gumptious	10* Cognizant	11 Equal	12 Progressing	13 Alert	14 Sincere
15 Neighborly	16* Provident	17* Humanitarian	18 Resolute	19 Geeky	20* Deductive	21 Loving
22* Sanguine	23 Inclusive	24 Elegant	25* Multi- faceted	26 Vigorous	27 Composed	28 Athletic
29 Tranquil	30 Freethinking	31 Bountiful				

"I AM

VOLUNTEERING.

It's about doing something, never 'nothing.'

I am that I am."

Hao Finley

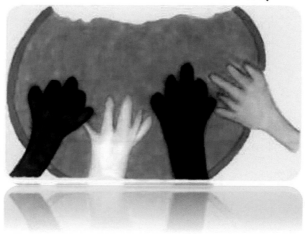

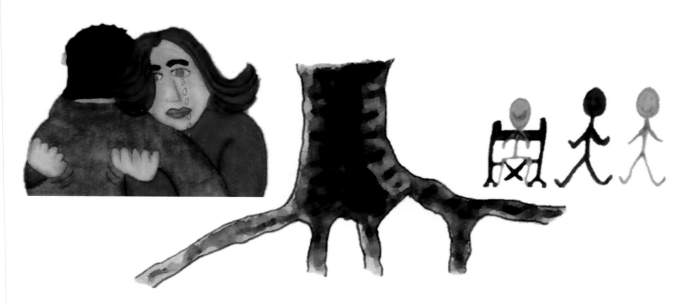

November

I AM _____ that I am.

I AM	I AM	I AM	I AM	I AM	I AM	I AM
1 Persistent	2 Logical	3* OM	4 Clever	5 Awakened	6 Encouraged	7* Jubilant
8 Amusing	9* Reputable	10 Inventive	11* Prolific	12 Collected	13* Diligent	14 Fit
15 Happy	16 Informing	17 Attractive	18* Grounded	19 Beaming	20 Thankful	21 Volunteering
22 Graceful	23 Forgiving but not forgetting	24 Cool- headed	25* Emboldened	26* Sociable	27* Revived	28* Munificent
29 Well- intentioned	30 Stimulated					

A+

"I AM

ACCOUNTABLE.

Blaming the dog is irresponsible.

I am that I am."

Sabine Yi, Hao Finley

"I AM **ENERGIZED.**
*Fellow philomaths, after some rest,
let's get organized."* Hao Finley, Sabine Yi

नमस्ते

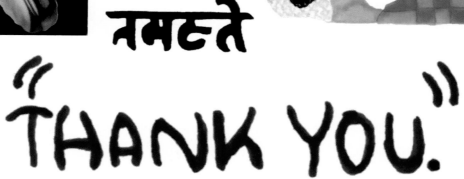

"THANK YOU."

December

I AM _____ that I am.

I AM	I AM	I AM	I AM	I AM	I AM	I AM
1 in Good Spirits	2 Joyful	3* Radiant	4 Achieving A+	5* Unruffled	6 Teeming (with...)	7 Cheerful
8 Helpful	9* Accountable	10* Philanthropic	11* Nimble	12 Breathing	13 Smiling	14* Vibrant
15 Peaceful नमस्ते	16 Warm-hearted	17* Diplomatic	18* Xenial	19* Acuminous	20 Caring	21 Feeling
22* Savvy	23 Imaginative	24 Kind	25 Merry	26 Quiescent for __ minutes	27 Owning my Power	28 Letting go
29 Complete	30 Energized	31* Appreciative "THANK YOU."				

About us

We love learning science and mathematics.

We read a lot of literature while trying to learn

languages with our mommy.

We play soccer and tennis too.

Other times we do yoga, which our daddy teaches us.

Fellow philomaths,

We'll be off on a long journey soon.

We'll give you a hint: it involves currencies, lots of it!

However, we will make a pit stop to collect some other vocabulary.

So, look out for HUMONGOUS (& Cool) Words for Kids soon!

You'll learn more about us there too.

Hope you continue with us in our pursuit of knowledge.

Please keep your I AM Manifesto close to you because

You ARE...that You are.

Hao Finley and *Sabine Yi (HF&SY)*

RYSS

GLOSSARY

January

(1) **Com.pas.sion.ate:** showing concern or sympathy for others and desire to help
(5) **Jo.vi.al:** friendly and cheerful
(6) **Stal.wart:** brave, valiant, hard-working, reliable, strong, loyal
(7) **Aus.pi.cious:** indicating a good chance of success or fortune; favorable; suggesting a positive future
(9) **Re.source.ful:** able to find quick, clever ways of dealing with problems
(10) **Com.pli.ment.ta.ry:** expressing praise, approval, admiration or respect
(14) **Qui.es.cent:** being in a state of rest or temporary inactivity; quiet
(17) **Per.cip.i.ent:** capable of or having a good understanding of things
(22) **Spry:** lively, active (*embracing this cool word to apply to a younger person*)
(28) **Zeal.ous:** showing or having zeal, ardently active or eager; devoted

February

(2) **Am.bi.tious:** having a strong desire and determination to succeed
(5) **El.o.quent:** clearly and effectively expressing something
(8) **Im.pas.sioned:** filled with or showing great warmth or emotion
(9) **Ver.sa.tile:** flexible; able to adapt to many different things
(18) **Dis.ci.plined:** having self-control
(19) **As.tute:** able to assess a situation or people accurately; discerning, shrewd
(24) **World.ly:** knowledgeable of many topics, sophisticated, cultured
(25) **Tact.ful:** careful not to say or do anything that could upset or offend others
(26) **Me.tic.u.lous:** very careful in attending to details; precise
(29) **Af.fa.ble:** sociable, good-natured, easy to talk to

March

(1) **Cir.cum.spect:** cautious, considering all circumstances and consequences
(3) **Fru.gal:** careful in spending money; thrifty
(8) **Daunt.less:** determined, fearless
(14) **Ju.di.cious:** having or exercising good judgment or sense
(15) **Wit.ty:** amusing in a clever way; full of clever humor
(20) **Fe.cund:** fruitful, producing an abundance of new growth; prolific
(25) **Re.sil.ient:** able to withstand or recover from a difficult condition or situation
(28) **Hos.pi.ta.ble:** welcoming and friendly to others; courteous
(29) **Al.tru.is.tic:** selfless, concerned for the well-being of others
(30) **Con.tem.pla.tive:** thinking deeply, or thinking in a serious and calm way

April

(1) **Gen.teel:** elegant, stylish, aristocratic, polishly-refined
(3) **Up.right:** honorable, respectable, honest, decent, ethical, having principles
(5) **Bliss.ful:** full of joy, extremely happy
(6) **Val.iant:** showing courage, brave, having valor
(7) **Em.path.ic:** able to understand or to be sensitive to the feelings of others
(9) **Come.ly:** pleasant to look at, attractive, handsome
(20) **Dis.creet:** circumspect, careful, not attracting a lot of attention
(23) **Sa.ga.cious:** showing or having good judgment
(24) **Ex.pe.di.tious:** acting or doing with speed and efficiency
(26) **Pa.cif.ic:** peaceful, calm, serene

May

(1) **Op.ti.mis.tic:** confident and hopeful about the future
(3) **Vo.cal:** outspoken; expressing myself freely and openly
(4) **Er.u.dite:** having or showing great knowledge or learning
(8) **Con.sci.en.tious:** guided by and wishing to do what is right
(12) **Dig.ni.fied:** serious and graceful in a manner that is worthy of respect
(13) **Zest.ful:** having great enthusiasm or energy
(17) **Pol.ished:** accomplished and skillful, masterly; cultivated
(20) **Em.pow.ered:** made stronger and more confident; liberated
(21) **Te.na.cious:** holding fast, tough, staying firm
(24) **Fruit.ful:** producing abundant growth; fecund

June

(3) **Ec.o.nom.i.cal:** not wasteful
(7) **Poised:** having a composed, elegant and self-assured manner
(8) **Mod.est:** humble, unassuming, unpretentious; free from vanity and ego
(9) **Com.pe.tent:** efficient, capable, adept
(10) **Ob.jec.tive:** even-handed, fair, just, impartial, neutral
(16) **At.ten.tive:** observant, paying close attention, perceptive
(17) **Dis.cern.ing:** having or showing good or careful judgment
(19) **Re.spon.si.ble:** having control over or care for something; answerable
(23) **Eq.ua.ble:** calm, even-tempered; not easily angered or disturbed
(24) **Jo.cose:** humorous, merry, playful
(28) **Ar.ti.san.al:** skilled in making something using traditional methods

July

(6) **U.nique:** one of a kind
(10) **Per.son.a.ble:** nice, have a pleasant manner, amiable
(12) **In.trep.id:** characterized by fortitude and endurance, fearless, adventurous
(16) **Ge.ni.al:** cheerful, easygoing, warm
(19) **Joc.u.lar:** humorous, playful, fond of joking
(22) **In.tu.i.tive:** able to know something without direct evidence or reasoning
(24) **Char.is.mat.ic:** charming, able to attract admiration of others
(25) **Ear.nest:** showing sincere and serious conviction
(27) **Gal.va.nized:** motivated to take action
(29) **Mag.nan.i.mous:** generous, courageous

August

(9) **Au.then.tic:** real, genuine
(12) **Blithe:** cheerful, happy, lighthearted
(17) **An.i.mat.ed:** lively, bubbly, excited, energetic
(19) **Per.spi.ca.cious:** having or showing keen understanding or discernment
(22) **Pros.per.ous:** having success in material terms; flourishing financially
(24) **Guile.less:** without deception, innocent
(26) **Dex.ter.ous:** skillful with my hands
(30) **Qui vive:** on the alert, vigilant
(31) **Tri.um.phant:** jubilant, being joyful or proud after a victory or success

September

(3) **Jo.cund:** cheerful, marked by mirth
(5) **Be.nev.o.lent:** kind to others, altruistic, doing good
(7) **No.ble:** upright, decent, ethical, magnanimous
(11) **Per.se.ver.ing:** pressing on or ahead; not taking no for an answer; holding on
(14) **Scru.pu.lous:** very careful to do things properly, thorough
(16) **Punc.tu.al:** on time
(17) **Guts.y:** showing courage, unafraid
(19) **Ce.re.bral:** intellectual
(23) **At.tuned:** able to understand, adapt or appreciate something
(24) **Un.flap.pa.ble:** calm in a crisis situation, not easily panicked or upset
(27) **Zip.py:** lively, bright
(28) **Pru.dent:** careful and thoughtful in providing for the future

October

(1) **Li.on.heart.ed**: brave, determined, fearless, gallant
(6) **Win.some**: appealing, attractive, generally engaging
(7) **Ur.bane**: sophisticated, worldly, cultured, suave, cultivated
(9) **Gump.tious**: shrewd common sense, resourceful
(10) **Cog.ni.zant**: being aware of
(16) **Prov.i.dent**: prudent, making provisions for the future
(17) **Hu.man.i.tar.ian**: concerned with improving people's lives; compassionate
(20) **De.duc.tive**: drawing conclusions based on logic and facts
(22) **San.guine**: optimistic especially in a bad situation, hopeful, ruddy
(25) **Mul.ti.fac.et.ed**: having many aspects, features or abilities

November

(3) **OM**: mantra, mystical sound of affirmation or assent
(7) **Ju.bi.lant**: feeling or showing great happiness or joy; rejoicing
(9) **Re.pu.ta.ble**: well-thought of, respectable, having a good reputation
(11) **Pro.lif.ic**: plentiful, inventive
(13) **Dil.i.gent**: showing care and seriousness in my work; conscientious
(18) **Ground.ed**: emotionally stable, sensible, realistic
(25) **Em.bold.ened**: given the courage or confidence to do something
(26) **So.cia.ble**: friendly, enjoy talking and being with other people
(27) **Re.vived**: given new energy; refreshed, rejuvenated
(28) **Mu.nif.i.cent**: generous, giving a lot

December

(3) **Ra.di.ant**: bright, glowing, gleaming
(5) **Un.ruf.fled**: composed, calm, untroubled, poised
(9) **Ac.count.a.ble**: responsible; expected to justify actions or decisions
(10) **Phil.an.throp.ic**: altruistic, humanitarian, generous, benevolent, charitable
(11) **Nim.ble**: agile, quick and light in movement; quick to comprehend
(14) **Vi.brant**: full of energy and life; dynamic, animated
(17) **Dip.lo.mat.ic**: able to deal with others in a sensitive and tactful way
(18) **Xen.ial**: hospitable, especially to visiting strangers
(19) **A.cu.min.ous**: sharp, keen
(22) **Sav.vy**: having common sense and good judgment; shrewd and knowledgeable
(31) **Ap.pre.cia.tive**: feeling or showing gratitude; thankful for

SB Hilarion is the author and main illustrator of the books behind the *Raising Young Scholars Series* featuring siblings Hao Finley and Sabine Yi. SB enjoys sharing new things that she learns, even with those who don't ask. After all, that's what a philomath would do. She lives with her husband and children, plus some groundhogs and deer who don't pay rent.

Maksym Turkot is a sixteen year-old artist who was born and raised in Lviv, Ukraine, where he currently lives. Inspired by his parents, who are both architects, Maksym developed his skills in drawing, composition, graphics, and sculpture at the Novakivsky Art School in Lviv. His fields of interest include sports, business analytics, statistics and biology, but art, being his passion, occupies a very special place.